DEDICATED TO MY FATHER PROFESSOR ALTAF HUSSAIN

Contents

Chapter 1: Introduction to Cost Accounting

I can imagine that the very first business activity which occurred on earth would be a barter trade, maybe it was an exchange of a bucket of rice with a bucket of wheat or a piece of meat? To analyse the fairness of the deal, both parties must have asked themselves" is the bucket of rice worth the same as the bucket of wheat?" At the times when there was no currency, it must be difficult to gauge the comparative values unlike now-a-day when we can find out the market value of any product easily and assess if one is striking a good deal or not.

So how would you assess a transaction like that in the old times?

One way to assess the above-mentioned barter trade, which I think is the most appropriate one, would be to think about how much effort was put into growing those two different crops, harvesting, and then further processing to make those seeds edible. If you know a few things about growing wheat and rice, you will know that rice is more resource intense to grow, e.g., it needs a lot more water than wheat etc. If I put myself into the shoes of the rice grower, I would say that it is not a fair deal to exchange a bucket of rice for a bucket of wheat as it took a lot more effort to grow rice. The efforts to grow rice (and wheat) are the **cost** of growing it and it can be concluded that the cost of growing rice is higher than growing wheat.

In the above scenario, I am not considering the taste and availability of the products from other parties, as this is a demand and supply issue rather than a costing one.

The above scenario created a branch of knowledge that we now call Accounting (cost accounting, to be more precise) and it may also suggest that the original/ initial function of accounting was to determine the cost of producing (or buying) and cost accounting is the original accounting. We can also derive a basic definition of cost from the above scenario which is "**cost** is the value of resources and efforts used or consumed in creating or producing a product or providing a service."

In the modern world, we simply put a monetary value to those resources and efforts which has made the modern complex trade possible. If you search online for the meaning of cost, one of the definitions is "an amount that has to be paid or spent to buy or obtain something" which is simpler than the one above as we have replaced efforts and resources with "money." The money we have earned and are carrying in our pockets or bank accounts is the cost of our time and efforts to the person or organisation for whom we work.

Traditionally, the **purpose of accounting (Cost)** was to deal with the costing i.e., determining the total cost of different products, services, and functions (e.g., departments) of the business. This was the time when reporting financial performance was not an objective of the accounting department. Financial Accounting which is the other main area of accounting discipline evolved later when calculation and reporting of business activities became a necessity (or legal requirement) for tax purposes and recently for corporate governance-related issues.

In the past, when businesses were small and producing only one or similar products (which would take similar efforts, time and material) and where organisational structure was simple, calculating the cost of a product was simple and it could be claimed that the total cost of the products/services could be calculated to a 100% accuracy.

However, nowadays, costing in even small businesses can be very complicated, rest aside the large manufacturing organisations which are producing 100s of different products. The organisational structures are also more complex with offices and manufacturing facilities in different countries and complex supply chains. There is no doubt that Cost Accounting has evolved to meet the needs of these complex organisations and dozens of new costing techniques have been invented including Activity-Based Costing, Process Costing, Target Costing etc. However, you will find this interesting that none of the methods would give us a 100% accurate cost of a unit of product/service in complex manufacturing organisations. Some are more accurate than others though, therefore, management should always strive to calculate the cost as accurately as possible. Although costing is not considered the main purpose of management, it can be a primary concern of the management to control costs. We usually use the word "control" with regard to the cost even though the ideal thing would be to reduce them. However, this is not possible all the time to reduce the cost, so the word "control" is more appropriate.

Why accurate costing is crucial?

Accurate costing can be very critical to the businesses' success and survival. Most of the time, the prices of the products and services are based on the cost of producing/ buying the products and providing the services. Many businesses have a standard mark-up percentage which they will add to the cost of the products to set the price of the product or service. A mark-up is an amount that is based on the cost of the products. For example, if a product is bought for £10 and the organisation policy is to charge a mark-up of 50%, the price will be fixed at 10+ 10x50%= £15.

If the cost of the product is calculated low which is a possibility if the business miscalculates/ignores (or simply forgets) certain costs to be added to the product's cost believing those costs are not relevant, the price of the product will be set lower than it should be which will result in the lower profits or even a loss.

If the price is set too high due to miscalculation of the cost, then the customers would go to competitors to buy the same or similar product. As management would always want to make some profit on each product they sell, they may not be willing to reduce the price to match competitors' prices. Hence businesses could be losing customers and profit due to incorrect costing. This scenario can be more likely in organisations where multiple products are beings produced/ bought and sold and/or services being offered. This miscalculation happens due to common costs which are not always easy to allocate to different products precisely. We will discuss these common costs in more detail in chapter 4 of this book.

So how do we ensure our costing is correct?

As mentioned above, Cost accounting deals with the determination of the cost of different products and functions of a business. Correct costing can be achieved by ensuring all costs which are being incurred in the business are accounted for.

For example. If you buy a product for £5, one might say that the cost of selling this product is £5, and if you set a price of £10 for it, you will be making a profit of £5. However, for most businesses in the modern economy, the cost of selling a product also includes

- Carriage inwards
- Cost of storage space i.e., warehouse costs
- Cost of handling i.e., warehouse staff
- Insurance costs
- Cost of obsolescence
- Interest cost etc

We will look at all possible costs, definitions and, their implications, in the next Chapter of this book.

Point to remember;

- **Cost** is the amount spent on creating or producing a product or providing a service.

- **Cost Accounting** deals with the determination of the total cost for different products, services, and functions of the business as accurately as possible.

- Accurate costing is crucial for businesses success and survival, but it may not be possible all the time.

- There are many different cost accounting techniques that would calculate the different total cost for the same product. Some techniques are more accurate than others.

Chapter 2: Costs Categorisation and Definitions

In this Chapter, we will discuss all types of costs that a business may have to incur which will help us to understand those costs. I usually say in my classes if you would like to control something (or someone then try to understand it first as understanding helps to control and the same applies to the costs.

Costs can be categorised by

1- Elements of a product/service
2- Direct or indirect link to a product/service
3- Functional and/or departmental costs
4- Correlation to the organisational activities i.e., fixed or variable costs

Elements of Costs

Classification of costs by its elements involves examining the products and services to identify different components of costs which were incurred to produce those products or providing those services. If we examine any product or service, we can easily identify different elements which require spending money to produce that product or provide the service. Labour and material costs are the most obvious ones which almost always exist in the cost structure. However, there are also other expenses which require a payment. For example, a car mechanic fixes your car by changing a part (material) which takes time (labour). However, the car mechanic also has to pay rent and other expenses for its workshop. Even if the mechanic is a mobile mechanic with no workshop, they still have to use a van and fuel to run their operations. This method of classification helps us to identify different costs while calculating the total cost. Accountants and management should be aware of all the costs if they want to calculate accurate costs, run their business efficiently and make effective decisions. Hence, this category will give us three types of costs;

i. Material
ii. Labour
iii. Expenses

The expenses usually cannot be directly identified with the products or services which a business sell. For example, it can be difficult to establish if any cleaning costs were incurred while manufacturing a product. These expenses may not relate to production and could have been incurred to run the other support functions of the business, for example, cost of running an office canteen. These are also known as "Overheads"

Total cost of any product or service will comprise of the above mentioned three elements. However, in the last 50 years the percentage composition of these costs has changed significantly. Before automation of the production processes I.e., production by robots and automatic production lines in factories, labour amounted to 50-70% of the total production cost. However, in modern production, the bigger chunk of total production cost is overheads as most of the labour work has been replaced by machines now, cost of running these machines fall under "expenses" category.

We will breakdown and examine overheads in more detail in section "Functional/departmental costs".

Direct or indirect Costs

This classification looks at each item of costs to ascertain if that specific cost is being incurred directly due to the production of a unit of product/service or if there is an indirect relationship of the cost with products and services. Direct costs are usually incremental costs which means the money is only spent on direct costs if another unit is produced or a service is provided. Ie times of inactivity, e.g., strikes or lockdowns during a pandemic, these costs can be avoided. Indirect costs or overheads (mentioned earlier as common costs) are usually the costs which will be spent anyway. This classification can help in decision making. For example, it can be identified how much extra will be spent by producing more.

It is worth mentioning here that indirect costs are the "**problem child**" of cost and management accounting. These are the costs which makes it difficult to determine the costs of different products with accuracy. Different organisations use different techniques to allocate these costs. Chapter 4 and 5 of this book will explore this issue in detail.

This classification gives us following categories of costs;

Direct and indirect material

Direct material is the material which can be identified from an individual product. This material is core to the product and the cost of it is significant to the total value of the product that can be accurately determined and attributed to the product. For example, a typical table in a classroom has two major materials used in it, wood and aluminium. These materials will be called direct material and cost of each material for each table will be calculated to determine the total cost of each table.

However, the same table may have other materials too which are not obvious or substantial but still cost money i.e., varnish, paint, screws, welding rods etc. These materials are called indirect as

1- The cost of these on each product is insignificant or immaterial to the total cost of the product. What is material or not is very subjective and different organisations have a different threshold (e.g., less than 5%) for all or each raw material

2- One box, bag or bottle of these materials is used on multiple products e.g., tables, chairs, desks etc

3- Most importantly, determination of the costs of these materials on each product will take more time (and money) than the cost saving or other benefits which can be obtained by accurately determining the cost of these materials on each product (cost v benefit analysis). In other words, we might be able to directly apportion these costs to different units which could result in increase in profits or decrease in costs by 2% but in doing so other costs will increase by more than 2%.

Therefore, indirect materials are grouped with other indirect expenses which are later allocated to each product using different methods under different accounting approaches. This will be discussed in detail in chapters 4 and 5 of this book.

Direct and indirect labour

Direct Labour is the cost which is directly incurred in making a Specific product or providing a service. This cost can be directly attributed to each unit/ service and calculated precisely. For example, in a factory which produces tables, chairs and desks, it can be observed how long it takes workers to cut, carve, assemble and finish a unit. The hour(s) can be multiplied with the rate per hour to calculate the cost of labour.

However, the same factory needs other staff who are not directly making those products but offering support services e.g.,

- a supervisor monitoring 50 workers manufacturing different products,
- cleaners cleaning the factory floor after every shift,
- security staff looking after the building etc.

These costs are not directly attributed to each unit due to the same reasons we discussed in direct material section plus it can be practically impossible to determine e.g., how much cleaning had to be done for table number 15 or chair number 45.

Direct and indirect expenses

Most of the expanses are indirect I.e., the money spent on those is generally for more than one type of product and consequently, these costs are divided among different products. Few examples of indirect expenses are

- Rent and rates
- Maintenance and depreciation (reduction in the value and life of) plant & machinery, buildings, motor vehicles etc
- Insurance
- Administrations costs
- Legal and professional fees etc

However, direct expenses are rare, exist only in few organisations and in project-based costing. Direct expenses are items of cost other than material and labour where cost incurred on those can be reliably measured and attributed to a specific unit of product or service.

To understand direct expenses, let look at two examples.

Example 2.1

Donna built a swimming pool in her house. She hired a specialist firm which specialises in this type of construction jobs. The construction firm owns diggers and other machinery which they use on various projects. In this scenario, direct expenses will be material and labour used to build the pool. Cost of machinery and other costs will be indirect costs.

Example 2.2

Ali, who is Donna's neighbour, also built a swimming pool. However, rather than hiring a specialist firm, he used his regular construction firm who has done couple of similar jobs in the past. The contractor will need to hire the machinery which will be used in building the pool. In this scenario, cost of hiring diggers and other tools specific to this job will be recorded as direct expenses.

Equations to remember;

> Total of direct costs is called Prime Cost=
> Direct Materials + Direct labour + Direct expenses

> Indirect costs are also called Overheads =
> Indirect Materials+Indirect labour+Indirect expenses

Functional/Departmental costs

Production and non-production costs are the major categories in this area. However, if an organisation does not produce but only buy and sell then it will not incur production costs.

Production costs

Production costs are those costs which are incurred when raw material is converted into finished and part-finished products. The followings are the sub-categories in this area.

- Direct Material
- Direct Labour
- Direct expenses
- Variable production overheads
- Fixed production overheads

We have already discussed direct material, labour and expenses so we will look at the last two items now.

Variable overheads and fixed overheads are the two elements of overheads. Their composition i.e., what costs are included in these expenses will depend upon

- the size of the business,
- if the business sells goods or services and
- which industry/sector a business is operating in.

However, in all cases some expenses will change in value (£, $ etc) on regular basis called "**variable overheads**" while others' value will not change (at least in the short-medium term) called "**fixed overheads**".

Variable production overheads

These are the indirect expenses which are incurred in the production facilities e.g., factories. These are called variable as the amount changes regularly usually due to the change in production level. For example, if production lines run for longer than more electricity will be consumed, machines will require more lubrication and maintenance, hence more oil (indirect material) and more engineers' time (indirect labour) will be needed. There will be more machinery breakdown requiring more parts replacements. Higher production will also require more quality testing and more batches produced will require more batch related activities including machine set ups, lines cleaning and clearing, test runs and sample testing etc.

Fixed production overheads

These are the indirect expenses which do not change in the short-medium term and the amount spent on those expenses does not depend on the volume of production. The followings are few examples of fixed production overheads;

- Factory rent & rates
- Factory insurance
- Factory building's maintenance
- Fixed salary staff who are not directly involved with production for example cleaning and security staff, supervisors and managers, storerooms and canteen staff etc

Non-Production overheads

Followings are the sub-categories in this area

Administrative costs

These are the costs incurred to run general admin of the business including head office rent and other building related expenses, head office staff salaries including directors and senior management, accountancy and legal department etc.

Selling costs

These costs are associated with promotion, marketing and sales related expenses including shop and supermarkets' rent and other building related expenses, shop managers and staff salaries, order receiving costs etc.

Distribution costs

If you have travelled on motorways in the UK (United Kingdom), you would have noticed massive buildings around motorway areas with the names of well-known UK businesses including Tesco, Sainsbury's, DHL etc. These buildings are distribution centres for these businesses where they receive deliveries from their suppliers (often directly from manufacturers), store and maintain those stock and deliver to shops and end customers. All expenses incurred to run those warehouses, for example, rent and other building related expenses, managers, drivers and staff salaries, lorries leases and fuel costs are all included in the distribution costs.

Finance Cost

In the modern economy, businesses often borrow money to establish i.e., building a new factory, warehouse or a shop and to run their operations. These loans require a payment of interest which is called finance cost. However, there are many businesses, especially the one following Islamic financing principles, do not take loans and hence will not have this type of cost.

Costs correlated to activity levels

This classification of costs segregates costs on the basis of how it reacts to the change in the level of business's operations i.e., producing and/or selling the products or services. The followings are the main classes in this category

Fixed costs

All those costs are fixed costs which do not change with the change in the level of activity (within a certain range) i.e., if a business produces/ sells more or less products. Examples for fixed costs are

- Rent & business rates
- Fixed salaried staff
- Building Insurance
- Telephone line rental
- Standing charges on gas and electricity connections etc

Example 2.3:

A factory has a capacity to produce 50,000 units per year. The annual fixed costs of this factory are £50,000 which includes rent, business rates, insurance and permanent staff salaries etc. Analyse the impact on this cost for various activity levels as below

- no production in the factory,
- produces 1 unit,
- produces 5,000 units,
- produces 25,000 units or
- produces 50,000 units.

As all the costs must be added to the total cost of production, the following amounts will be added to the cost of production in different scenarios given above

Fixed costs	Production units	Fixed costs per unit	
£50,000	-	-	£50,000/0 units
£50,000	1	£50,000	£50,000/1 units
£50,000	5,000	£10	£50,000/5,000units
£50,000	25,000	£2	£50,000/25,000units
£50,000	50,000	£1	£50,000/50,000 units

Following points can be noted from the above table

- Pre-production costs are added to the cost of building factory (capitalised) and will not be added to the cost of producing goods.

- Fixed costs are capped at £50,000 no matter how much is produced (within the capacity)

- Cost per unit decreases as the production increases. Therefore, management will always seek to produce to full capacity to make products more competitive and profitable.

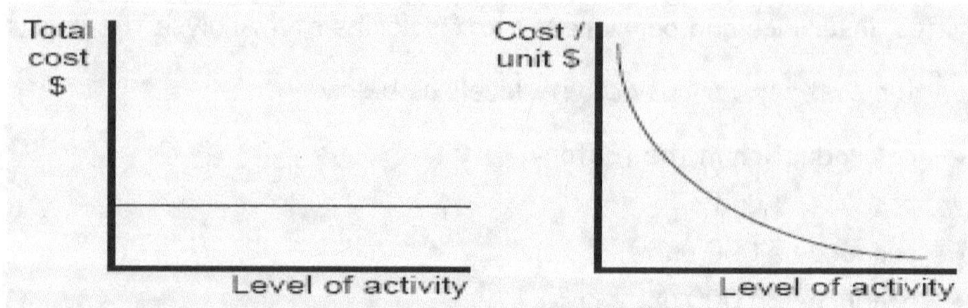

The above graph (left) shows **total fixed costs** as a straight line on horizontal axis when the activity is increasing but costs do not change. The graph on the right shows the drop in **per unit fixed costs** as the activity increases.

Stepped fixed costs

We discussed above that fixed costs do not change within a certain range i.e., capacity limit. What happens when capacity of the factory is exceeded i.e., the business needs to produce more than 50,000units? This question brings us to a well understood viewpoint that all costs are variable (semi-variable) in the long-term. Fixed costs are fixed within a given range and then it increases. However, increase in the fixed costs is not a gradual one but it usually jumps or takes a step up. For example. In example 2.3, when the same business needs to produce more than 50,000 units, the production facilities need expansion. At this stage, the management of the business need to evaluate by how much they need to expand their production facility. There could be two scenarios

1- The growth in business orders is limited and/or unsustainable
2- The business will keep growing in future

A logical solution to deal with option 1 would be to extend the existing factory. Let's say that an extra line of 10,000 units is added to the current production capacity. There will be an increase in the fixed costs but not a proportionate one. Maintenance and depreciation of machinery will cost additional money and there may be a need to hire more personnel but there will be no increase in the rent & rates. Let's say this additional capacity will cost £5,000 per year. This will make the cost to jump from £50,000 to £55,000 irrespective of how much of the additional 10,000 production capacity is utilised.

If option 2 (continuous growth) is more probable, then it will be better to build a new factory altogether rather than extending the existing one. Let's say a similar factory is built which will cost the same amount in fixed costs as the first one. In this case the fixed cost will jump from £50,000 to £100,000. Even if the business produces only 25,000 units in the second factory. This shows how fixed costs increase in steps unlike a variable cost as we will discuss next. The same increase occurs when other fixed costs need additions for example, hiring another supervisor on a fixed salary, opening another shop etc.

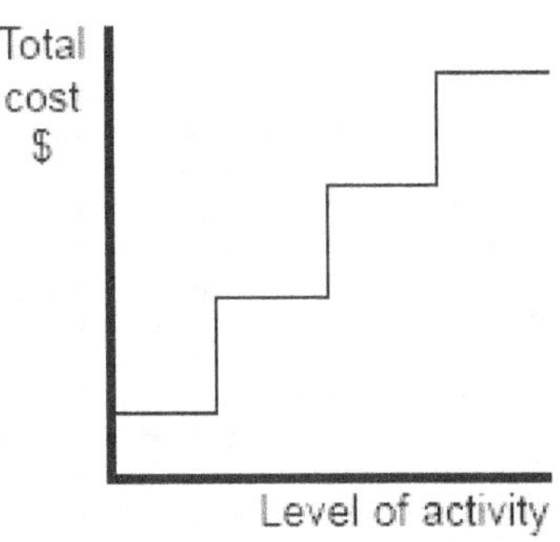

<u>**Variable cost**</u>

A variable cost is a cost which changes with the change in the level of activity and the change in cost is in the same proportion as the change in activity. This means an increase of 50% in the activity will increase the cost by 50% too. Cost per unit for variable cost will remain same at different activity levels (within a given range, obviously).

Example 2.4:

A table requires 2 meters of wood and 4 kg of aluminium to produce. The cost per meter of wood is £5 and 1 kg of aluminium costs £10. The total cost of material on the table would be

		£
Wood	2mx£5	10
Aluminium	4kgx£10	40
Total material cost		50

The second table will cost the same money on wood and aluminium and so on. The number of tables increased by 100% (from 1 to 2) and cost also increased by 100% (from £50 to £100). As the production increases, total variable cost will increase but cost per unit will remain the same.

Table units	Cost per table	Total cost
1	£50	£50
2	£50	£100
10	£50	£500
200	£50	£10,000

The same will apply to the cost of labour. These (material and labour) are the two major variable costs.

The graph below (left) shows how variable cost reacts to the change in level of activity (e.g., production). A straight line represents proportionate change in cost when the activity changes. The graph on the left shows that variable cost per unit remains the same when activity changes.

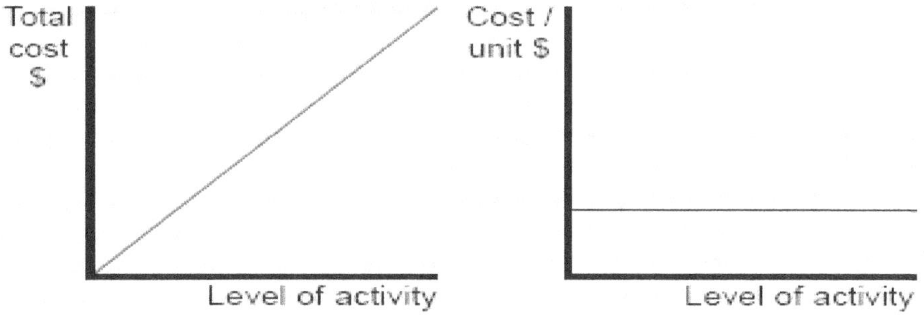

Let's assume that if the same manufacturer produces more than 10,000 tables, it can secure a 5% discount on the material due to bulk buying which would result in reduction in the per unit cost.

Should this reduction be applied to the units produced below 10,000 unit? The answer to this question depends on the contract with the suppliers. If the discount is applied to previous purchases too then it will be applied to all production which is usually the case as most of the purchasing is done on credit and an adjustment can be made at the point of payment.

Should this reduce the price of the products too? Management should consider the impact of increase in production on other costs before deciding on this. An opposite impact can happen with labour. As the demand increases, labour cost will increase due to supply of skilled labour and trade union related issues which can push the total cost of production higher.

<u>Semi-Variable/ Semi-fixed Cost</u>

These are the costs which have an element of both fixed and variable cost to it. As a result, a part of these costs remains fixed when the activity changes while the other element changes as a variable cost would do. The total cost will change when the production/activity increases like a variable cost but the cost per unit will not be the same as it is the case with variable costs.

For example, most of the utilities in the UK have a fixed element of cost called standing charges which means a fixed amount will be payable even if the customer does not use the service at all. The cost of variable element depends on the usage, for example, KWH of electricity or Gigabits of data. For many businesses, labour cost is also semi-variable/fixed as they would employ permanent as well as per hour and zero hours contracted employees which are used when the production or other activities exceed a certain level.

From management viewpoint, the whole purpose of understanding costs is to enable them to control these costs, plan for the future and make better decisions. It is well understood that fixed costs cannot be managed in the short-medium term, but variable costs can be reduced quickly if needed. However, semi-variable costs pose a challenge in their raw form as the impact of a decision cannot be evaluated on these costs with precision. Therefore, these costs are segregated into fixed and variable costs to know the exact amount of fixed and variable amount in a certain total for a cost e.g., total payroll cost or production costs.

Example 2.5

Kiev Ltd produces sunflower oil in one of its factories. Production overheads for January were £10,000 for 5,000 units and in February were £16,200 for 9,000 units. Analyse the production overheads into variable production overheads and fixed production overheads.

Solution:

We can see that the total cost has increased from £10,000 to £16,200 displaying a characteristic of a variable cost. At this stage, we cannot assume that production overheads include any fixed costs.

However, a main test of variable cost is that it keeps the cost per unit same at different levels. So, let's check if production overheads given are fully variable or there is also an element of fixed cost into it. This can be achieved by calculating cost per unit at two given levels of activity.

Activity - units	Total cost	Cost per unit
5,000	£10,000	£10,000/5000= £2.00
9,000	£16,200	£16,200/9,000= £1.80

As the table shows, the cost per unit has changed and decreased. If you can remember from example 2.3, the cost per unit decreased as the activity increased which means production overheads are displaying a characteristic of fixed costs too. This proves that production overheads are a semi-variable/fixed cost. Once it is known that a cost is semi-variable, it should be segregated into its fixed and variable elements for better decision-making. For example, this information can inform us total production overheads at 15,000 units to prepare cash budget for future. This can be achieved by using High-Low Method.

High-Low Method.

This method uses two different activity levels, a high and a low, with their respective total costs to determine variable cost per unit using the equation

$$\text{Variable Cost per unit} = \frac{\text{Change in costs}}{\text{Change in activity}}$$

The logic is that when the activity changes from a low level to high level, the costs increase but as fixed costs do not change with the change in activity, the increase only comes from increase in the variable cost. Hence the change in cost is all variable which can be divided by the change in activity (units etc) to find out variable cost per unit. Let's apply this logic to our example above.

$$\text{Variable cost per unit} = \frac{£16200 - £10,000}{9,000 - 5,000} = \frac{£6,200}{4,000} = £1.55$$

Once we know variable cost per unit, we can find out fixed costs by using this equation

$$\text{Fixed Costs} = \text{Total Costs} - (\text{Variable Cost per unit X number of units})$$

To get the figures for total cost and number of units, we need to pick an activity level from the data set (out of two in this case), any one activity will serve the purpose as we will see later. I will pick the low activity in this case with total cost of £10,000 and activity level of 5,000 units. Let's put these figures in the above equation now.

Fixed costs = £10,000 – (£1.55 x 5,000 units)
Fixed costs = £10,000 – (£7,750) = £2,250
Now we have segregated production overheads of £10,000 into

Variable cost = £7,750
Fixed cost = £2,250

Check

Activity level of 9,000 units

I have stated above that we can pick any activity level and we should be able to get the same fixed cost. Total variable cost would obviously be different as it depends on the activity level. Let's see if we get the same fixed cost at a higher activity level. As per the definition of fixed cost, we should get the same value.

$$Fixed\ Costs = Total\ Costs - (Variable\ Cost\ per\ unit\ X\ number\ of\ units)$$

Fixed costs = £16,200 – (£1.55 x 9,000 units)

Fixed costs = £16,200 – (£13,950) = £2,250

Now we have segregated production overheads of £16,200 into

Variable cost = £13,950

Fixed cost = £2,250

How to use this information for future planning?

Once we know variable cost per unit and total fixed cost for the organisation, we can work out the total costs for any given level of activity using the equation below

$Total\ Cost = Fixed\ Costs + Variable\ Cost\ per\ unit\ X\ number\ of\ units)$

Example 2.5.1

Kiev Ltd is expecting to produce 15,000 units in March due to high demand. However, management is worried that they may not be able to produce enough to meet the demand due to limited finances. Most of the sales made by Kiev Ltd are on credit. Management accountant is estimating the finances required to apply for a short-term loan to meet the demand. One of the estimates required is for factory production overheads.

Solution:

Total Cost   = 2250 + (1.55x 15000)
               = 2250 + 23250 = £25,500

Similarly, production overheads can be calculated for the entire year which will be useful to construct a cash budget for the whole year.

This concludes our chapter on introduction to costs. In the coming chapters will discuss why we need to know all this information and how it can be used.

<u>**Test your knowledge with multiple choice questions**</u>

1.   Which of the following best describes a variable cost? A cost which:
        a. Has a direct relationship with output
        b. Remains at the same level year after year
        c. Represents a fixed proportion of total costs
        d. Remains at the same level when output increases

2.   A business's telephone bill should be classified into which one of these categories?
        a. Fixed cost
        b. Stepped fixed cost
        c. Semi-variable cost
        d. Variable cost

The data below relates to the questions 3-5.

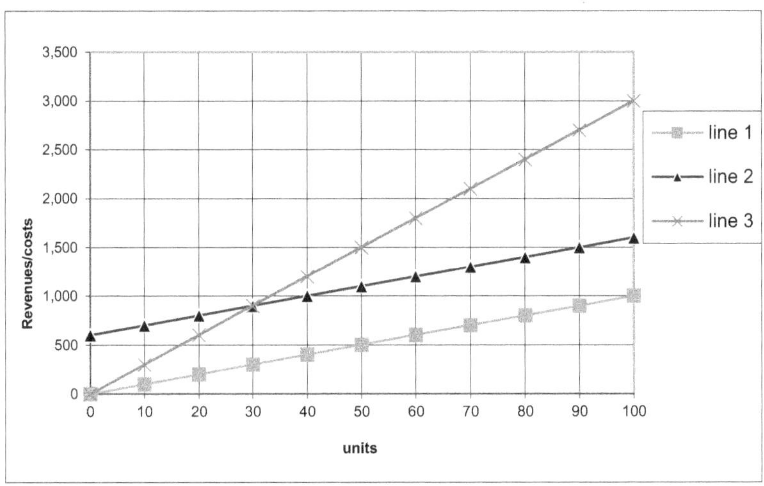

3.   In the above graph which one of the following describes Line 1?
        a.   Fixed costs
        b.   Variable costs
        c.   Total costs
        d.   Total revenue

4.   In the above graph which one of the following describes Line 2?
    a.   Fixed costs
    b.   Variable costs
    c.   Total costs
    d.   Total revenue

5.   In the above graph which one of the following describes Line 3?
    a.   Fixed costs
    b.   Variable costs
    c.   Full costs
    d.   Total revenue

6.   Which of the following is a direct cost?
    a.   Factory heating bill
    b.   Depreciation on machinery
    c.   Manufacturing wages
    d.   Administration salaries

7.   Variable costs are usually considered to:
    a.   Be constant per unit of output.
    b.   Vary per unit of output as activity changes.
    c.   Be constant in total when the level of activity changes.
    d.   Vary, in total, from period to period when production is constant.

8.   A salesperson is paid a basic salary plus commission for each sale made. This wage cost is a:
    a.   fixed cost.
    b.   variable cost.
    c.   semi-variable cost.
    d.   production cost

The data below relates to the questions 9-10.

B plc provides a call centre service to a number of utility and financial services customers. It has four separate call centre buildings plus a head office. Many of the telephone staff are students and casual employees who are paid weekly, on an hourly basis. Their contracts state that B plc has no duty to provide them with work. The telephone staff are managed by permanent supervisors and managers. Although there are no direct material costs as such, the company incurs telephone charges which are directly related to the number of calls it handles. There is a central computerised exchange which routes the calls received.

9.   Which of the following costs would you classify as fixed costs?

1. Lease charges for the buildings
2. Telephone staff costs
3. Supervisor and management costs
4. Telephone charges
5. Computer exchange lease costs

    a. (1), (3) and (4)
    b. (2) and (4)
    c. (1), (3) and (5)
    d. All of them

10.   Which of the costs would you classify as variable costs?

    a. (1), (3) and (4)
    b. (2) and (4)
    c. All of them
    d. Only 4

11.   Which of the following would be classified as indirect costs for a car manufacturer?

    (i) Maintenance materials used to repair production machinery
    (ii) A maker's badge on the boot lid
    (iii)Cleaner's wages at the factory

a. (i) only
b. (i) and (iii) only
c. All of them
d. None of them

12.   A company makes one delivery per week to its customers. The cost of these deliveries is:

a. A direct production expense
b. A prime cost.
c. A production overhead.
d. A selling and distribution cost.

13.   Indirect costs and overheads are synonyms terms True or False?

a. True
b. False

14.   Which one of the following statements is true?

a. Total direct costs are always greater than total indirect costs.
b. Indirect costs are alternatively called overheads.
c. Fixed costs per unit are the same at all levels of production.
d. A direct cost will always be a fixed cost.

15.   Finance Cost can be classified as non-production cost. True or False?

     a.   True
     b.   False

16.   Which of the following costs is not a production costs?
     a. Direct material
     b. Direct labour
     c. Variable production overheads
     d. Distribution costs

17.   Which of the following can be classified as production costs?
     a.   Admin Costs
     b.   Selling costs
     c.   Distribution costs
     d.   Direct Expenses

Questions on High Low Method

The data below relates to the questions 18-22.

	Activity level	
Costs	2000 units	5000 units
Supervision	£20,000	£20,000
Direct material	£100,000	£250,000
Storage & handling	£10,000	£17,500

18.   Which of the cost can be classified as variable?

     a. Supervision
     b. Direct material
     c. Storage & handling
     d. None of the above

19.   Which of the cost can be classified as semi-variable?

    a.   Supervision
    b.   Direct material
    c.   Storage & handling
    d.   None of the above

20.   What is the variable cost per unit for Direct material?

    a.   £1.00
    b.   £2.50
    c.   £50
    d.   £100

21.   What is the variable cost per unit for Storage & handling?

    a.   £1.00
    b.   £2.50
    c.   £50
    d.   £100

22.   What is the fixed cost in the total cost for Storage &
handling?

    a.   £10,000
    b.   £17,500
    c.   £2,000
    d.   £5,000

23.   The total production cost for making 20,000 units is £40,000
and the total production cost for making 50,000 is £52,000. So, the
variable cost of making one unit is:

    a.   30 p
    b.   40p
    c.   50p
    d.   60p

24.   B plc has estimated that its overheads will be $250,000 next year if it handles 1,000,000 calls, and $280,000 if it handles 1,250,000 calls. What will its overheads be if it handles 1,100,000 calls?

   a. $275,000
   b. $268,000
   c. $262,000
   d. $246,400

The following data relates to the questions 25-27.

The cost of making 5,000 units is £14,000 and for 10,000 units is £17,000.

25.   What is the variable cost of making one unit?
   a. 30 pence
   b. 40 pence
   c. 50 pence
   d. 60 pence

26.   What are the fixed costs of the business?
   a. £5,000
   b. £7,000
   c. £9,000
   d. £11,000

27.   Using the data from question 25 and 26, what will be the total cost of producing 15,000 units?
   a. 15,000
   b. 18,000
   c. 20,000
   d. 25,000

The data below relates to the questions 28-30.

Rooney Ltd provides a single standard service. The business's results for the past two months are as follows:

	April	May
Sales (units of the service)	500	620
Sales revenue (£)	25,000	31,000
Operating profit (£)	10,000	14,800

28.   What was total cost in April?

    a. £10,000
    b. £25,000
    c. £15,000
    d. £50,000

29.   What was variable cost per unit?

    a. £10
    b. £15
    c. £20
    d. £25

30.   What was the fixed costs?

    a. £10,000
    b. £25,000
    c. £15,000
    d. £50,000

Answers to these questions can be found at the end of this book.

Chapter 3: Costing

Costing is a process of identifying, accumulating and quantifying all costs which are incurred in relation to a cost object, cost unit or a cost centre.

Cost object: any activity for which a separate measurement of cost is undertaken, e.g., a set for a movie or an exhibition

Cost unit: a unit of product or service in relation to which costs are ascertained e.g., a mobile phone or a room in a hotel.

Cost centre: a production or service location, function, activity or item of equipment for which costs can be ascertained e.g., a programme of study in a university

Costing will produce a document called "Cost Card" which will list all the costs incurred on a cost unit, object or centre.

Cost Card

Once we know all the costs which will be incurred to produce and sell a unit of product or service, a cost card will be produced for that product or service. A cost card for a cost object, unit or centre brings together all the costs relating to it and gives total cost for it. Below is an example of a typical cost card.

	£
Direct Material	X
+Direct Labour	X
+Direct Expenses	X
=Prime Cost	XXX
+ Variable Production Overhead	X
=Variable Cost of Production	XXXX
+Fixed Production Overhead	X
=Total Production Cost	XXXXX
+Non-production Overhead	X
=Total Cost of a Unit	XXXXXX

However, depending upon the complexity of a business, the cost card may look different and include different labels and costs. For small businesses with simple operations, cost card may look simpler than the above example.

To build a cost card, all costs must be identified and quantified. Quantification of direct costs is usually a straightforward thing as costs is easily identifiable and measurable and managers with some arithmetical skills should be able to calculate these costs. However, as mentioned in the previous chapters, indirect costs are the real problem in costing and understanding how to quantify those costs for different products can be a real challenge even for qualified cost accountants. To calculate accurate overheads for each product, there are several techniques available and different organisations use different techniques to do so. In the next few chapters, we will look at two costing techniques which calculate indirect costs to be added to a cost card in different ways.

Chapter 4: Absorption Costing

Absorption costing is the original technique to deal with indirect costs, therefore, it is also called "Traditional Costing." This method can be a simpler way to allocate overheads to products and services in practice although it can give inaccurate figures allocated to different products and services in complex manufacturing scenarios. In my experience, students find this method confusing as there is no fixed rule to deal with overheads. Accountants in different organisations use their own judgement on how best to divide the common costs i.e., overheads among different products and services.

To understand absorption costing, imagine that overheads are a bucket full of water and products/services being produced are sponges on a moving line. Each sponge (unit) will absorb some water in such a way that the last sponge produced will absorb the last bit of water from the bucket. How much each sponge absorbs will depend on the size of the sponge (material), how long it stays in the bucket (hours) and other issues like absorbability of the sponge (skills required, quality of material, quality control, machinery required and so on).

Absorption costing uses a hypothetical "basis" to absorb the overheads into different products. An assumption is made that all indirect costs are incurred due to a reason called "basis of absorption (BOA)." Total units of BOA (e.g., unit, hours etc) are established which are used to calculate "Overheads Absorption Rate (OAR)." An OAR is a unit with a monetary value (£, $ etc) in which total overheads are divided. The following formula is used to calculate OAR

$$OAR = \frac{\text{Total Overheads}}{\text{Total units of BOA}}$$

The most obvious basis (reason) is the "number of units" i.e., the business has spent money on rent, rates, electricity, cleaning, maintenance etc because it was producing units (e.g., cars) in its production facility.

Example 4.1:

Teska Inc. produces electric cars in one of its production facilities in Shanghai. Total overheads for a period are $370 million and the production was 21,700 cars. If number of units is used as basis (denominator) than overheads calculations per car would be as follows

Overheads per car = \$370,000,000/21,700

= \$17,051

This means \$17,051 will be added to each car's production cost to calculate total production cost of each car. Assuming the material cost per car was \$8,500 and labour cost is \$4,600 per car, we can calculate the total production cost for each car as below

	\$
Direct Material	8,500
Direct Labour	4,600
Production Overheads	17,051
Total Production cost	**30,151**

This method of absorption is only acceptable and correct if the factory is producing only one model of the car or different models which take same efforts to produce, and pricing of the products is similar. An OAR like this is called a **blanket OAR**. This is the easiest way to allocate overheads to different products.

However, if an organisation produces products which use production resources in significantly different proportions, then a blanket OAR will lead to incorrect cost calculation to different products/services.

Example 4.2:

Teska Inc. produces 4 different models called S, E, X, Y in its Shanghai factory. The prices and direct cost information is given below

Model	S	E	X	Y	Total
	$	$	$	$	
Price	85,000	45,000	150,000	57,000	
Direct Material	17,000	8,500	29,750	10,200	
Direct Labour	5,800	4,600	13,800	5,060	
Units (Cars)	1,200	7,150	350	13,000	21,700

From the information above, we can see that different models are costing different amounts on direct material and direct labour. If a car requires more material, then it requires more storage space to keep that material in the stores, it requires more handlers, management time, etc. Higher direct labour cost means that it took longer to produce which means more electricity was used to run machinery, lighting, maintenance and so on. If we equally divide the total overheads among these products, then it will not be a fair and correct allocation of the overheads. Therefore, the unit of production basis is not an appropriate basis in this case. Remember that although there is no fixed way of allocating overheads in absorption costing, basis of absorption must be the one which will allocate the costs fairly and appropriately among different products/models. A 100% correct allocation will not be possible in the above scenario using absorption costing due to the complexity of the operations. To deal with a situation like this, other basis of absorption should be selected. It is usually the one which is more resource intense or where the resource is limited in supply. For electric cars, material is in limited supply so maybe it is a better basis of absorption? However, direct material does not have a direct link with many costs incurred in the factory.

It can be determined how long it takes to produce each car with precision so may be labour hour is the most appropriate basis of doing it? In reality, accounting softwares could be asked to do various calculations using different basis and final results would need a judgement call from management to decide which basis is more appropriate. I think now you should be able to see why absorption costing is confusing ☺.

Example 4.3

Let's further explore the above example to see how different basis can have an impact of cost distribution among different products. The table below gives more data per car.

Model	S	E	X	Y	Total
Price $	85,000	45,000	150,000	57,000	
Direct Material $	17,000	8,500	29,750	10,200	
Direct Labour $	5,800	4,600	13,800	5,060	
Direct Labour hours per car	290	200	500	253	
Machine Hours per car	150	70	350	75	
Units (Cars)	1,200	7,150	350	13,000	21,700

From the information given in the above table, various OARs can be calculated using different BOAs as below

4.3.1 Overheads absorption on the basis of cost of material:

The assumption is that money was spent on overheads because organisation was buying, storing, and using the material to produce products. In most cases, the weight or volume of the material is the more appropriate basis but if you can understand money spent on a material basis, you should be able to understand the logic to apply it on other bases of absorption.

$$\text{OAR} = \frac{\text{Total Overheads}}{\text{Total money spent on material}}$$

$$= \$370,000,000/\ 224,187,500*$$

$$= \$1.65$$

*Total money spent on material

Model	S	E	X	Y	Total
Direct Material $	17,000	8,500	29,750	10,200	
Units (Cars)	1,200	7,150	350	13,000	
Total Direct Material Cost $,000	20,400	60,775	10,412	132,600	224,188

This means that every $ spent on material will cause $1.65 worth of overheads and if a car costing $1 on material, then it should be absorbing $1.65 worth of overheads. For example, Model S overheads will be calculated as 17,000 x 1.65 = $28,057 as given in the table below along with overheads for other models.

Profit per car for each model with material cost as BOA

Model	S	E	X	y
	$	$	$	$
Price $	85,000	45,000	150,000	57,000
Direct Material $	17,000	8,500	29,750	10,200
Direct Labour $	5,800	4,600	13,800	5,060
Overheads	28,057	14,025	49,088	16,830
Profit per Car	**34,143**	**17,875**	**57,363**	**24,910**

A check can be done to see if all the overheads has been absorbed by all products or not as the table below shows

Overheads per car $	28,057	14,025	49,088	16,830	
Cars	1,200	7,150	350	13,000	
Total Overheads $,000	33,668	100,279	17,181	218,790	370,000

4.3.2 Overheads absorption on the basis of direct labour hours:

This is one of the most commonly used bases to absorb overheads into the cost of products. To calculate OAR using labour hours, we will need to calculate total labour hours in the factory which are calculated in the table below

Note: Total labour hours have been calculated by multiplying labour hours per car with units of each car (e.g., for model S - 290x1200).

Model	S	E	X	Y	Total
Direct Labour hours per car	290	200	500	253	
Units (Cars)	1,200	7,150	350	13,000	21,700
Total Direct Labour hours (000s)	348	1,430	175	3,289	5,242

$$\text{OAR} \quad = \frac{Total\ Overheads}{Total\ labour\ hours} =$$

$$=\$370{,}000{,}000/5{,}242{,}000 = \$70.58$$

This means that every labour hour will cause $70.58 worth of overheads and if a car using 1 labour hour, then it should be absorbing $70.58 worth of overheads. Model S overheads will be calculated as 290 × $70.58 = $20,469 as given in the table below along with overheads for other models.

Model	S	E	X	Y	Total
Direct Labour hours per car	290	200	500	253	
OAR $	70.58	70.58	70.58	70.58	
Overheads per Car $	20,469	14,117	35,292	17,858	
Units (Cars)	1,200	7,150	350	13,000	
Total Overheads per model $,000	24,563	100,935	12,352	232,150	370,000

Total cost per car for each model with direct labour hours as BOA

Model	S	E	X	Y
	$	$	$	$
Price $	85,000	45,000	150,000	57,000
Direct Material $	17,000	8,500	29,750	10,200
Direct Labour $	5,800	4,600	13,800	5,060
Overheads	20,469	14,117	35,292	17,858
Profit per Car	**41,731**	**17,783**	**71,158**	**23,882**

4.3.3 Overheads absorption on the basis of machine hours:

Most modern production facilities use automated lines, and, in many cases, the biggest proportion of production overheads is dependent on how many hours (machine hours) these lines are run in a period. In such cases, machine hours are the most appropriate basis of absorption. We will now calculate OAR using a machine hours basis with the same information we have used in the previous calculations

Model	S	E	X	Y	Total
Machine Hours per car	150	70	350	75	
Units (Cars)	1,200	7,150	350	13,000	
Machine Hours per model	180,000	500,500	122,500	975,000	1,778,000

$$\text{OAR} = \frac{Total\ Overheads}{Total\ machine\ hours}$$

$$=\$370,000,000/1,778,000 = \$208.10$$

This means that every machine hour will cause $208.10 worth of overheads and if a car has used 1 machine hour, then it should be absorbing $208.10 worth of overheads. Model S overheads will be calculated as 150 x $208.10= $31,215 as given in the table below along with overheads for other models.

Model	S	E	X	Y	Total
Machine Hours per car	150	70	350	75	
OAR $	208.10	208.10	208.10	208.10	
Overheads per Car $	31,215	14,567	72,835	15,607	
Units (Cars)	1,200	7,150	350	13,000	
Total Overheads per Model $,000	37,458	104,154	25,492	202,897	370,000

Total cost for each model with machine hours as BOA

Model	S	E	X	Y
	$	$	$	$
Price $	85,000	45,000	150,000	57,000
Direct Material $	17,000	8,500	29,750	10,200
Direct Labour $	5,800	4,600	13,800	5,060
Overheads	31,215	14,567	72,835	15,607
Profit per Car	**30,985**	**17,333**	**33,615**	**26,133**

The table below presents a comparison of overheads distribution and

profit or loss on each product under different absorption basis.

		Material Cost	Labour Hours	Machine Hours
S	Overheads $	28,057	20,469	31,215
	Profit Per Car $	34,143	41,731	30,985
E	Overheads $	14,025	14,117	14,567
	Profit Per Car $	17,875	17,783	17,333
X	Overheads $	49,088	35,292	72,835
	Profit Per Car $	57,363	71,158	33,615
Y	Overheads $	16,830	17,858	15,607
	Profit Per Car $	24,910	23,882	26,133

Each insurance cost should be apportioned on the level of risk basis e.g., which departments can cause more damage to the building due to vibrations, fire etc? Which department has expensive equipment? Or which department involves riskier work for employee insurance. Accident records can be used to determine the percentage insurance which can encourage managers to take actions to reduce accidents as this will reduce the cost apportionment to their department.

There will be many other costs needs apportionment and different organisations may have different bases for all of the costs. The discussion above should be enough to give you an idea of the issue and why this exercise may be a critical part of a manager's job.

Example 4.5

The table below gives a breakdown of Teska Inc Overheads for a period and the basis which should be used to apportion the overheads to different departments in the factory.

Teska Inc	$millions	Basis of absorption
Indirect labour	200	Direct labour hours
Machine depreciation	70	Machine hours
Building maintenance & depreciation	50	Floor area
Lighting and heating	5	Floor area
Material handling and storage	45	Material cost
Total Overheads	**370**	

You can see that overheads and profit figures for each product are different with different BOAs. It cannot be determined with certainty which absorption basis gives the most accurate values for overheads; however, the management of the business (with the help a of management accountant) will be able to choose the most appropriate basis. Other possible bases of absorption could be the percentage of prime cost, material weight, volume or length, percentage of skilled labour cost, etc. It can be a difficult decision to choose a single basis for the whole factory when different bases are important in different departments. In such scenarios, rather than having just one OAR, various departmental OARs are calculated which make the calculations more complicated but more accurate apportionment and allocation of overheads can be achieved.

Departmental Basis of Absorptions

Modern production facilities usually have multiple departments e.g., stores, cutting, assembly, finishing and packaging etc. for a furniture-making factory. The working methods can vary, and a production factor can have different significance in different departments. Therefore, a different BOA should be chosen for each department. For example,

- Stores can absorb its overheads on the basis of how much space material takes,

- Cutting department can be based on machine hours assuming it is automated or primarily machine based,

- Assembly department can be based on direct labour hours if majority of work is carried out by human
- Finishing department overheads could be absorbed on the basis of skilled labour hours
- Packaging department can absorb its overheads on the basis of cost of packaging material, if that is significant, or labour cost if packaging is carried out by labour

Example 4.4

Teska Inc. factory in Shanghai has the following departments and departmental overheads

	Stamping	Plastics	Paint	Assembly	Body	Total
Departmental Overheads $millions	66.00	39.15	27.75	160.50	76.60	370.00
Machine hours(millions)	0.80	0.09	0.27	0.36	0.27	1.78
Labour hours(millions)	0.26	0.52	0.26	3.14	1.05	5.24
Material cost $million	67.26	40.35	26.90	17.94	71.74	224.19

We can see from the above data that the Stamping department is using most of the machine hours and it is likely that the most appropriate BOA is machine hours in the Stamping department. The Assembly department is labour-intensive and labour hours should be BOA in that department. Material cost is very significant in three departments i.e., Stamping, Plastics and Body. Both Plastics and Body could use this as

BOA while The Stamping department has another contender for BOA. The management will need further information to decide on BOA and the above is only a simplified version of decision-making in this area.

As we have established, choosing a BOA is entirely subjective but the aim is to distribute the common costs (indirect costs) to the products as accurately as possible. Each departmental manager will make this decision on the basis of their judgement with the help of data given from management accountant.

Departmental Overheads Absorption Rates

A different BOA in each department which will lead to different departmental OARs. The formula to calculate OAR will slightly change as below

$$Departmental\ OAR = \frac{Departmental\ total\ Overheads}{Departmental\ BOA}$$

The above formula suggests that we need to understand how departmental Overheads are calculated so we can have both variables for the formula.

Apportionment of common overheads to departments

In the previous section, we modified the formula to calculate departmental OAR and by replacing total overheads with total departmental overheads in the numerator. Calculating total factory overheads can be a simple task as it can be done by adding up all the bills etc. However, calculating departmental overheads can be a big challenge in real life. This is not just because of arithmetical issues but there are also social issues which make this task burdensome. Although there will be many items of costs which can be directly associated and allocated to different departments, e.g., departmental managers and staff salaries, maintenance and depreciation of department's assets etc, there are always costs which are paid for the whole factory or business which will require dividing and allocation to different departments e.g., rent, rates, building insurance, lighting and heating, security staff, etc. This process is called "apportionment of common overheads" which is carried out by using a basis of apportionment.

This apportionment should be fair however, fairness is quite a subjective thing. A basis deemed reasonable by one manager may not be suitable for another manager. As departmental managers always try to keep their departmental costs low, any basis which would increase their departments costs in a bigger proportion then other departments will not be acceptable. Below are the examples of common overheads which may require apportionment to different departments. We will discuss how these should be apportioned and why a basis may be more suitable in each case.

Rent, rates, lighting, and heating/air conditioning:
These costs arise due to the size of the building. It will be logical to apportion these costs on the basis of how much space e.g., square meters or square feet, each department is occupying. This can enhance efficiency in space usage and can reduce these costs in the long run as all managers would try to use as less space as possible to avoid getting

extra costs. It is assumed here that heating and air conditioning is centralised in this case. Some departments may require extra air conditioning costs, for example, IT as servers require cooling down, therefore, this cost may be apportioned on the electricity usage basis rather than the area occupied.

Electricity:

This cost should be apportioned on the basis usage which can be measured by installing internal meters. However, if that is not possible then a good estimate should be made. Departments which are machinery intense will use a lot more electricity even if it occupies less area.

Machine Depreciation:

This is one of the biggest indirect costs in the businesses where production is automated. The total cost of installing the machines is spread over the life of the machines and a portion of the total cost is included in the yearly costs over the life of the machines. It is logical to spread this cost on the basis of value of the machines in each department. Departments which rely heavily on machines will get a bigger proportion of this cost.

Insurance:

There are various types of insurance that a business may have to pay for e.g., Building insurance, contents/ Machinery and equipment insurance, employee, and customers insurance etc.

The basis of apportionment data is given below in the table

Departmental data	Stamping	Plastics	Paint	Assembly	Body	Total
Floor area %	20.00	8.00	5.00	40.00	27.00	100.00
Machine hours	0.80	0.09	0.27	0.36	0.27	1.78
Labour hours	0.26	0.52	0.26	3.14	1.05	5.24
Material cost $million	67.26	40.35	26.90	17.94	71.74	224.19

Using the information above, we can apportion the overheads to different departments as below

Teska Inc	Departmental Overheads				
All amounts in $millions	Stamping	Plastics	Paint	Assembly	Body
Indirect labour	10.00	20.00	10.00	120.00	40.00
Machine depreciation	31.50	3.50	10.50	14.00	10.50
Building maintenance & depreciation	10.00	4.00	2.50	20.00	13.50
Lighting and heating	1.00	0.40	0.25	2.00	1.35
Material handling and storage	13.50	8.10	5.40	3.60	14.40
Total Overheads	**66.00**	**36.00**	**28.65**	**159.60**	**79.75**

Workings

Apportionment of Indirect Labour cost		
Teska Inc	$millions	
Stamping	10.0	200*0.26/5.24
Plastics	20.0	200*0.52/5.24
Paint	10.0	200*0.26/5.24
Assembly	120.0	200*3.14/5.24
Body	40.0	200*1.05/5.24
	200.0	

Apportionment of overheads to Stamping Department			
Teska Inc	$millions	$millions	
indirect lab	200	10	200*0.26/5.24
machine dep	70	31.5	70*0.8/1.78
building maintenance and dep	50	10	50*20/100
lighting and heating	5	1	5*20/100
Material handling and storage	45	13.5	45*67.27/224.19
Total Overheads	370	66	

The above workings should enable you to understand how this apportionment was calculated.

After determining BOA and calculating total overheads for each department, OARs can be calculated. Departmental overheads will be absorbed into each product as we have done above for the whole factory. The cost card will change to reflect absorption of overheads by different departments as below

Model	S	E	X	Y
	$	$	$	$
Price $	85,000	45,000	150,000	57,000
Direct Material $	17,000	8,500	29,750	10,200
Direct Labour $	5,800	4,600	13,800	5,060
OVERHEADS				
Stamping	X	X	X	X
Plastics	X	X	X	X
Paint	X	X	X	X
Assembly	X	X	X	X
Body	X	X	X	X
Total Production Cost	Xxxxx	Xxxxxx	Xxxxxxx	xxxxxx

<u>**Test your knowledge with multiple choice questions**</u>

The following data relate to questions 1 and 2.

Delta Plc produces three products and has traditionally used a costing system which absorbs the overheads based on direct labour hours which are currently 88,000 hours.

The following overheads cost figures are from the current year;

	£
Set up costs	30,000
Order receiving costs	1,195,000
Packing	250,000
Engineering	373,000
Total overheads	1,848,000

The direct costs per unit for products X, Y and Z are;

	X	Y	Z
Direct Labour (£)	8	12	6
Direct Material (£)	25	20	11
Units Produced	30,000	20,000	8,000

The labour cost is £6 per hour.

1. What is the total cost of producing product X?

    a. £61

    b. £74

    c. £38

    d. None of the above

2.   What is the total cost of producing product Z?

   a. £61
   b. £74
   c. £38
   d. None of the above

The following data relates to the question 3-6.

Ali Baba Ltd uses absorption costing to allocate overheads to its three products X, Y and Z. Overheads are absorbed into products on machine hour basis. Total production overheads for the period are £720,000. Direct labour cost is £8 per hour. The Table below gives the data relating to the individual products;

| Products | Hours/unit | | Material cost/unit | Volumes |
	Labour hours	Machine hours	£	Units
X	1	2	10	1500
Y	1.5	3	20	4000
Z	2	3.5	24	6000

3.   What is the total number of machine hours to produce all the units of three products?

   a. 40,000
   b. 50,000
   c. 36,000
   d. 46,000

4.   What is the overhead absorption rate?

  a. 10
  b. 15
  c. 20
  d. 25

5. What is the total cost for one unit of X?

  a. 10
  b. 58
  c. 66
  d. 19

6. What is the total cost of one unit of Z?

  a. 110
  b. 58
  c. 158
  d. 10

Answers to these questions can be found at the end of this book.

Scenario based question

A boat manufacturer produces different sizes of boats. A small boat requires £300 worth of wood. An operator works for 5 hours in the machining department to cut the wood as per specifications. This material is then sent to Assembly department where two workers assemble the boat in one shift of 8 hours. Total Overheads and activities in each department were as below;

	Total Overheads	Machine Hours	Labour Hours
Machining department	£200,000	5,000	1,000
Assembly department	£150,000	-	10,000

The labour rate is £20 per hour in both departments.

Required: Calculate the total production cost of the boat. Use absorption basis which is more suitable in each department.

Solution

			£	£
Direct Materia				300
Direct labour	Machining department	5 x £20	100	
	Assembly department	16 x 20	320	420
Prime cost				**720**
Overheads	Machining department	5 x £40 (w1)	200	
	Assembly department	16 x £15 (W2)	240	440
Total production cost				1160
Working 1	£200,0000/5000 Machine hours	40		
working 2	150,000/10,000 Labour hours	15		

Chapter 5: Activity-Based Costing

Activity-Based costing (ABC) is a relatively new method of calculating total cost for products and services. Although in the classroom exercises and exam questions, this method may seem similar to Absorption Costing, in practice it is very different and much more precise technique than absorption costing.

ABC records all activities in an organisation and links those to products or services which is causing each activity to occur and causing costs to increase. This enables the management accountants to add different costs to different products and/or services resulting in accurate cost calculations unlike in Absorption Costing where overheads are first put together and then allocated and apportioned on the basis of an activity (e.g., labour hours) which is selected subjectively.

It is immense work to record all the activities in an organisation and link those to different products and/or services which has only been made possible with the widespread use of information technology since 1990s. The activities are monitored by using computers without causing disruption to the work processes. Unlike Absorption Costing which relies on departmental OARs to allocate overheads to the products and services, ABC uses Cost pools and cost drivers to achieve precision in overheads allocation and apportionment.

Cost Pools and Cost Drivers

In absorption costing, we have looked at how overheads are accumulated for each department and then departmental OARs are calculated. Cost Pools are similar to departments in this regard. However, where there are only few departments in an organisation, there could be 100s of Cost Pools in each organisation which helps to narrow down the costs to link them to the right product or service. **Cost pools** are the total cost (£, $ etc) of the similar activities e.g., administration department. This similarity is usually established by the cost driver of each activity. A **cost driver** is a variable which causes costs to increase in a cost pool e.g., hiring a new person in admin department etc. This cost driver will trigger admin department to become a cost pool as there is cost associated with it. Once total value for cost pools and total number of drivers are known in each cost pool, a rate per driver is calculated using the formula below

$$\text{Rate per Cost Driver} = \frac{\text{Total Cost in Cost Pool}}{\text{Total number of Cost Drivers in the cost pool}}$$

ABC will record number of drivers for each product which will be multiplied with rate per driver to calculate the cost which should be added to a product from that cost pool. This will be repeated for all the cost pools which were associated with that product. This will give us the total overheads cost for each product. By adding material and labour cost we can calculate the total cost for a product.

Cost Card using Activity-Based Costing				
Model	S	E	X	Y
	$	$	$	$
Direct Material $	17,000	8,500	29,750	10,200
Direct Labour $	5,800	4,600	13,800	5,060
Overheads				
Admin	X	X	X	X
Human Resources	X	X	X	X
Marketing	X	X	X	X
Machining	X	X	X	X
Stores	X	X	X	X
Distribution	X	X	X	X
Quality Control	X	X	X	X
Batch related	X	X	X	X
Ordering	X	X	X	X
Building related	X	X	X	X
R&D	X	X	X	X
Finance cost	X	X	X	X
Other Costs	X	X	X	X
Total Production Cost	Xx,xxx	Xxx,xxx	Xxx,xxx	xxx,xxx

The below are few examples of Cost Pools, their associated cost drivers, and an explanation of how ABC allocates overheads for each cost pool.

Departmental cost pools:

Most of the departments including admin, marketing, HR, R&D, finance will be a cost pool as there are costs which can be clearly associated and accumulated in there. The possible cost drivers could be

Cost Pool	Cost Driver	Cost allocation
Admin	Number of staff or staff hours	ABC will monitor how many people/ hours worked for each product/service. Costs will be apportioned on that basis
Marketing	Number of staff or marketing campaigns	ABC will monitor how many people/ hours worked for each product/service, or how many marketing campaigns were run for each product/service and Costs will be apportioned on that basis. Actual spend on each product can also be monitored.
Human Resources	Number of staff or staff hours, staff hired	ABC will monitor how many people/ hours worked for each product/service. Or how many people were hired/ trained for each product. Costs will be apportioned on that basis
Research & Development	Actual spent on each product/service	ABC will monitor how much was spent on each product/service.

Finance		ABC will monitor how many people/ hours worked for each product/service. Costs will be apportioned on that basis

Machines related costs:

This cost pool accumulates all costs related to running and maintaining machines in an organisation. For example, machine depreciation, lubrication, maintenance and repairs, parts, engineers' salaries, and any other machine related cost excluding new machine purchases which are not overheads but capital expenditures.

Batch related costs:

Imagine a Coca-Cola Factory where products are produced with different volumes, containers, and flavours. Total demand for each product is produced in smaller chunks rather than in one go. For example, if the demand for 500ml bottle is 100 million in the UK, it is likely that it will be produced, let's say, 10 times throughout the period. Producing the whole lot will be foolish as it can cause massive problems like storing the product, investment stuck in stock for the whole year, products getting out of date and so on. Each production run is called a batch. Every time a different batch is run, machinery requires resetting, whole system needs flushing to avoid flavours getting mixed, filters changing and so on. These costs are accumulated in a pool and apportioned on the basis of how many batches each product required. A Product with more batches but smaller quantities will receive higher costs, hence more expensive to produce. For example, 10 batches of 500ml bottles produced in the quantity of 100 million will be allocated the same batch costs as 10 batches of Coke Vanilla 330ml with a total production of 1 million.

Ordering and distribution costs:
This includes staff costs involved with taking and processing orders. ABC will record the number of staff/hours worked for each product. The costs will then be apportioned accordingly.

Distribution costs:
These costs include warehouse costs, workers and managers dealing with receiving and dispatching deliveries, maintaining stock, delivery trucks and associated costs etc. These costs will be monitored by ABC to identify how much was spent for each product.

Building-related costs:
These costs include rent, rates, insurance, maintenance, depreciation, and other building related costs. Usually these are apportioned on the same basis as absorption costing which is floor area occupancy. However, ABC can allocate costs to this cost pool more accurately.

Other costs:
After allocating all the costs to different cost pools, there will always be few items of costs which will be either too small to be made a separate costs pool or too unique to become a part of another pool. These costs are put together and apportioned using the same philosophy as Absorption Costing. The critics of ABC use this to criticise this technique. However, the difference is that Absorption

costing allocates 100% of the overheads using a basis whereas ABC does this to a small proportion (5-10%) of the overheads. If the proportion is too high, then either ABC system was not devised properly, or it should not have been implemented in the first place. As implementation of ABC requires significant financial investment, a Cost-Benefit Analysis must be carried out before implementing it.

Cost-benefit Analysis.

Implementing ABC is a huge decision which management should not take lightly. For medium to large size organisations, ABC's implementation can cost in $millions, disrupts the current processes and can cause social issues among staff e.g., anxiety and reluctance to change. Systems like ABC are implemented by management consultant firms which provide a plan for the implementation giving full details of what it will involve including costs for equipment, redundancies, further hiring and consultancy fees. A total figure must be calculated to establish the total cost of the new system.

The consultant reports also highlight the possible advantages of implementing the new system. However, the management must always exercise their own judgement on the matter as consultants are trying to sell their services after all and their reports could be biased.

The main advantage which ABC can bring to an organisation is accurate costing of different products and/or services which can make a business more competitive. ABC can identify the products and/or services which are more resource intensive as it monitors all activities in the organisation and links those to different products and/or services. Such information can help management to decide if they should continue providing a certain product/service or not if it is not making enough profits. A decision to drop a product can help management to focus on more profitable products and services and may reduce staff costs as well. A decision can also be made to increase the prices of those products if possible. On the other hand, prices could be reduced for the products/services which are cheaper to produce than originally calculated under the traditional costing method which will increase the sales and market share. In some cases, competition can be eliminated by enhanced processes like ABC. All the possible advantages must be calculated and accumulated to get a final figure for the benefits which can be derived by implementing ABC.

Total cost figure will be calculated and compared to the total benefits figure and a decision to implement the new system will only be made if the benefits exceed the costs. In some cases, social aspects of change can be so huge that the decision is still a NO even if the benefits exceed the costs. However, if a change is occurring throughout the sector, then management has no option but to implement the new systems as the business may not be able to survive if they don't embrace new systems and processes. Almost all the big companies have now implemented ABC in some form or another. Global competition has forced businesses to reduce costs to stay in business which is only possible with a robust costing system like ABC. Many businesses were shocked to find out the real costs of providing their products and services after implementing ABC where they were selling some of the products for less than the cost calculated under ABC while in some cases the prices were set too high based on traditional costing methods resulting in smaller market share. However, the research has also shown that some businesses did not find ABC useful to reduce costs and/or increase profits.

1. Which one of the following is NOT true of ABC?
   a. ABC stands for Action Biased Contribution
   b. ABC attempts to precisely allocate overhead based on the real factors that create costs
   c. ABC uses cost drivers
   d. ABC has been developed to supplement or replace absorption costing

2. Which method provides better costing information?
   a. Absorption costing
   b. Activity-based costing
   c. Marginal costing
   d. Relevant costing

3. Implementation of Activity-based costing is a simple process
   a. True
   b. False

4. Cost drivers accumulate similar costs
   a. True
   b. False

5. Activity-based costing and absorption costing produce similar total costs for products and services
   a. True
   b. False

6. Activity-based costing has proven effective in all the organisations
   a. True
   b. False

Answers to these questions can be found at the end of this book.

Question 1

E Ltd provides four types of services to their customers, details of which are as follows;

Product	Fox	Aero	Wax	Sox
Selling Price (£)	800	600	780	450
Labour Cost (£)	160	80	320	120

E Ltd uses activity-based costing to allocate general overheads to each service. The information on the cost pools, cost drivers and total costs are given below;

Cost Pools	Total Cost per pool	Cost Pool drivers
Administration costs	598,500	No. of customers
promotion costs	259,910	No. of staff involved
building related costs	1,299,375	Square meter occupied

The following information relates to the cost drivers for each service;

No. of Cost Drivers	Fox	Aero	Wax	Sox
No. of customers	1500	1200	2100	900
No. of staff involved	30	18	33	13
Sq. meter occupied	500	300	700	150

Required:
   A. Calculate a cost driver rate for each activity.
   B. Calculate total overheads per service and per customer using Activity Based Costing.
   C. Calculate the total profit per customer for each service using Activity Based Costing.

<u>**Solution**</u>

A.

First find total number of drivers for each cost pool as below

No. of Cost Drivers	FOX	AERO	WAX	SOX	Total
No. of customers	1500	1200	2100	900	5700
No. of staff involved	30	18	33	13	94
Sq., meter occupied	500	300	700	150	1650

Then calculate cost driver rate as below

Cost Pools	Total Cost per pool	No. of Cost Drivers	Cost Driver rate
Administration costs	598,500	5,700	105.00
promotion costs	259,910	94	2,765.00
building related costs	1,299,375	1,650	787.50

B.

Calculate overheads per product by multiplying rate per driver with drivers per product. For example, for Fox, administration costs will be apportioned as 105*1500 (rate per driver*number of drivers which fox caused in administration costs pool)

	FOX	AERO	WAX	SOX
Administration costs	157,500	126,000	220,500	94,500
promotion costs	82,950	49,770	91,245	35,945
building related costs	393,750	236,250	551,250	118,125
Total overheads per product	634,200	412,020	862,995	248,570
Customers	1500	1200	2100	900
Overheads per customers	422.80	343.35	410.95	276.19

D. Profit per customer

	FOX	AERO	WAX	SOX
Selling Price £	800	600	780	450
Labour Cost (£)	160	80	320	120
Overheads	422.80	343.35	410.95	276.19
Profit	**217.2**	**176.65**	**49.05**	**53.81**

Question 2

P Ltd makes two products, Bin and Win. Information relating to each of these products is set out below.

	Bin	Win
Selling price per unit	£52	£91
Annual sales volume	15,000 units	18,000 units
Number of sales invoices	200	800
Labour time per unit	2 hours	5 hours
Labour rate per hour	£10	£10
Material cost per unit	£25	£30
Size of each production batch	750	1,000
Bought-in parts per unit	2	1
Machine set-ups per batch	2	5
Total cost of production (absorption costing)	49	90

The finance director of P Ltd has recently produced the following analysis of overheads and their relevant cost drivers.

Type of overhead	Cost driver	£
parts handling costs	Number of parts	96,000
Materials handling costs	Number of batches	38,000
Sales invoicing costs	Number of invoices	20,000
set-up costs	Number of set-ups	26,000
All other overheads	Labour hours	60,000
Total overhead costs		**240,000**

Required:

Calculate the total cost per unit and profit per unit for each product using the activity-based costing method.

<u>**Solution**</u>

Total number of drivers

Overhead Activity	Cost driver	Cost drivers Bin	Cost drivers Win	Total cost drivers
Parts handling costs	Parts	15,000*2= 30,000	18000*1= 18,000	48,000
Materials handling	batches	20	18	38
Sales invoicing	invoices	200	800	1,000
set-up	set up	40	90	130
Other Labour	labour hours	15,000*2= 30,000	18,000*5= 90,000	12,000

Rate per driver

Overhead Activity	Total Cost driver volume	Total Overhead cost	Driver rate
Parts handling costs	48,000	96,000	2
Materials handling	38	38,000	1,000
Sales invoicing	1,000	20,000	20
set-up	130	26,000	200
Other Labour	12,000	60,000	0.5

Overheads per product= number of drivers *Driver rate

Overhead Activity	Bin	Win
Parts handling costs	30,000*2=60,000	18,000*2=36000
Materials handling	20*1,000=20,000	18*1,000=18,000
Sales invoicing	200*20=4,000	800*20=16,000
set-up	40*200=8,000	90*200=18,000
Other Labour	30,000*0.5=15,000	90,000*0.5=45,000
Total Overheads per product	**107,000**	**133,000**
Number of units	15,000	18,000
Overheads per unit	7.13	7.39
Direct costs		
Labour	2*£10=20	5*£10=50
Material	£25	£30
Total Costs per unit	£52.13	£87.39

Chapter 6
Target Costing

We have discussed earlier in this book that one of the main reasons for calculating total cost of a product/ service is to establish a price for it. Many organisations produce a product, establish the total cost, and then add a mark-up to set a price for their products.

Well – that's what used to happen but not anymore in many sectors. After globalisation in 2005, the competition has become fierce in the business world. Same (or similar) product can be bought from many different suppliers with competing prices. In the current environment, producers need to establish the prices for their product/services which a market is willing to pay before they even produce it. If the market is unwilling to pay the price set and required by the business, then the business will have three choices

1- Reduce the mark-up on the product
2- Abandon the idea/product
3- Reduce the production cost of the product

In most of the cases, organisations have a standard mark-up which they will add on their products/services. The management would not be willing to reduce the mark-up to reduce the price as this will divert their time from the products which may already be generating desired mark-up. There could be other future products/ideas which can fetch the desired mark-up.

For big companies like Uniliver or Tesco, abandoning a product may not be an issue but for some companies like Airbus, Apple, Audi, or tesla it can be a major issue. For such companies abandoning a product may mean leaving a whole sector for competitors who can steal company's market share in other products consequently. An example is Ford which is forced to sell electric vehicle at a loss as it does not want Tesla to monopolise this sector.

If the management, decides to go ahead with the project, then they will work backwords (from a set price to the required cost rather than from a set cost to the required price) to reduce the cost of the product to a level where the product can be sold at the price which a market is willing to pay and desired profit is also achievable. This approach is called **Target Costing**.

In some cases, small adjustments in the product may reduce the cost to the desired level. This may involve reducing the weight, volume, size and/or functionality of the product minutely which consumer will not notice.

There is another option available to the management to reduce production cost before deep diving into Target Costing which is **outsourcing** the production of the product. Many countries where cost of production is too high due to factors like high labour cost, rent, rates, and insurance etc are producing products in the developing countries including China, Vietnam, Thailand, India, Bangladesh, and Pakistan etc. However, it is not always possible to outsource due to issues like unavailability of technical skills in the developing countries, protection of patents, company policies etc.

Target costing approach pushes management out of the box to find the solutions to reduce the production cost. As we have discussed in chapter 2 of this book, variable costs are the one which can be reduced in the short term so the management focus will be on material and labour costs which are two most prominent types of variable costs.

Reducing the cost of material:

Most obvious solution would be going back to the supplier and renegotiating the prices of the raw materials. Many profitable businesses get negligent in this area as there is no genuine push to decrease the prices of the inputs. However, if management knows they need to reduce the cost of the raw material, say by 15%, they will try hard to get this reduction from their supplier. If current suppliers agree to reduce the prices, then the problem is solved. Otherwise, the business will be forced to look for other suppliers in the market.

Finding new suppliers may bring more opportunities for the business, not only for the product in question but also for other products. Existing suppliers may have been arranged a long time ago and the business may not have looked harder for better prices elsewhere.

To arrange new suppliers, the business will require quotations from all the suppliers in the market. The competitive pricing may bring higher savings than required which will be beneficial for the business and the product will generate even higher return.

However, it is not always possible to find new suppliers for some raw materials due to limited competition and suppliers in the market. For example, electronic industry is facing chip shortage after covid-19 pandemic and there are not enough suppliers to meet the demand. The raw material may not be available from other parties due to copyrights of the raw material.

Another solution would be to use the raw material of a reduced quality if it will not have a significant effect on the saleability of the product. For example, there are many touch screen tablets in the market which use lower quality raw materials including the touch screens to compete in the market. However, lower quality material has an adverse impact on the quality of the product (an obvious one), increased raw material wastage, quality inspections, product rejection rate and product returns. Therefore, a decision to reduce raw material quality should not be taken lightly. Poor quality material also increases labour cost as labour finds it harder to work with cheap quality material and more production is needed due to higher rejection rate.

Reducing the Cost of labour:

Many businesses have their own production facilities now in the developing countries to enjoy the benefits of cheap labour. This is different than outsourcing as outsourcing involves hiring another business to produce for you. If the business already has overseas production facility, then it must have already been included in the original costing, therefore, this solution does not apply in this situation. However, if a business does not have overseas facility, then this could be considered if the new product is expected to be sold in large quantities. This will be a huge decision which must be evaluated properly using various decision-making techniques which management accounting offers. This could reduce the production cost significantly not only for the proposed product but also for existing and future products. However, a post-covid phenomenon is increased in the shipping costs which has five-folded in some cases. This is a point which goes against outsourcing and overseas production. Many US and European companies have already started thinking about returning to in-house production as excessive shipping costs have made overseas production not worthwhile.

Another option to reduce labour cost is to use semi-skilled or low skilled labour instead of skilled labour which can reduce the cost of production. Although, this option increases material wastage, for some industries it has proven successful option to reduce the costs. In my student life I was working in a factory in West London producing CDs and DVDs for Hollywood movies. The students were working at the minimum wage while the permanent staff was getting three times more pay for the same work as they were considered skilled due to their experience at the factory. That factory closed down few years later anyway due to changes in the industry and competition from overseas. Labour cost can also be decreased by negotiating with labour unions. If a business is facing fierce competition which is threatening its existence, labour union may be willing to accept reduce pay which can reduce the costs of its products. Many businesses reduced staff pay during pandemic to reduce the costs for their survival.

Target Costing: An Example

Micola Inc developed an electric car to rival Teska Inc's electric car model E. The estimated figures on price and cost are as below

	$
Price	40,000
Material cost	12,500
Labour cost	8,000
Overheads	15,000

Profit per car	4,500

Micola Inc wants to keep the price below Model E as it wants to attract customers. Although both cars have the same battery range and specifications, market research has revealed that Micola's car has better aesthetics. However, customers have doubts on the reliability of the data given by Micola especially on battery range and life. Expected sales are 1,000 per month in comparison to model E which has monthly sales of 7,150. However, if the price is dropped to $35,000, Micola can expect to sell 5,000 cars per month. Although profitability is not Micola's objective in the short-term, it desires to keep it at around $5,000 per car as a safety margin, in case prices of the raw material increase in near future and if they have to further reduce prices to attract customers. It expects to decrease the production cost as production increases achieving economies of scale. Micola has decided it will not go ahead with production if it cannot sell the car at break-even in the short-term.

The above results from market research led the management to reduce the price to $35,000 with an objective to capture biggest market share with smaller profit per car.

Further investigation via focus group revealed that there are certain car features which can be removed without affecting customers' experience of the car who would be willing to accept 15% less battery range at a price of $35,000. These adjustments can decrease the material cost by 12% while the labour cost will be reduced by 10%.

There are no savings in the overheads. The estimated figures after using target costing are as below

	Original estimates	Target Costing approach
	$	$
Price	40,000	35,000
Material cost	12,500	10,625
Labour cost	8,000	7,200
Overheads	15,000	15,000
Profit per car	4,500	2,175

Although there is still a profit per car, it is less than desired profit of $5,000. The margin of safety is very small and a small increase in the prices of raw material will make this product unprofitable. On the upside Micola will have a bigger market share.

Should Micola go ahead with the car production?

What other factors you would consider before making a decision?

The answers to the above questions are not simple and same for different organisations. Managers have to make decisions all the time in uncertain scenarios like above and better decisions could be made with experience (which comes after making mistakes), gut feelings and a bit of luck.

Chapter 7: Other Costing Techniques

The topics covered so far in this book are sufficient for a manager to understand costing, its process and related wider issues which a manager should be aware of about cost accounting. However, there are other costing techniques which are important to be aware of as a manager. Detailed discussion on these is not deemed necessary as it does not fall within the scope of this book which is to introduce managers to cost accounting rather than to make them expert in all the costing techniques available. The below are the brief introduction to other well-known costing techniques.

Marginal Costing: This costing method is mostly used for decision making rather than to calculate total cost of the products. Although under certain scenarios it may be the best technique to be used for costing. Marginal costing ignores fixed costs and uses an extremely important concept called "Contribution towards fixed costs and profit" shortly called "contribution" which is calculated by subtracting variable costs from price of the product/service.

Relevant Costing: Broadly speaking, this costing technique fall within the scope of Marginal Costing principles. It uses important decision-making terminologies including opportunity cost and sunk cost. This costing technique is used for one-off projects or jobs.

Job Costing: This costing technique is used to calculate the total costs of a one-off project or job and to give a quotation. Any costing technique principles can be used i.e., absorption costing, relevant costing, depending upon organisations' regular costing technique.

Batch Costing: We have already discussed in chapter 6 what a "batch" is and what type of costs are involved in batch production. This costing technique is used to calculate the total cost of each batch produced.

Process Costing: A very complicated costing technique which is used in industries where various products are produced from the same raw material, e.g., an oil refinery, involving multiple production processes. The aim of this costing technique is to add the correct costs to each finished product.

Standard Costing: This is a very important control technique available to management. It helps to understand the reasons behind the differences between the budgeted (standard) and the actual results across different functions/departments of the business.

The above is not an exhaustive list of the costing techniques. Different industries and sector use different costing techniques as per their suitability. It takes time for the managers to understand the terminologies and the report produced by each costing technique. Therefore, don't panic if you hear or read a costing terminology or technique which you have never heard of after joining an organisation. Management Accountants are there to support and help you to understand the costing processes, reports it produce and make effective decisions.

<u>Summary of the book</u>

Absorption costing: (or full costing) an accounting method that calculates the costs of a product or service by adding together all the costs - fixed as well as variable - and dividing by the number produced.

Activity-based costing (ABC): a costing approach originally devised by Kaplan and Cooper in the 1980s, which is intended to bring about a better understanding of overheads and to create a more efficient form of cost control. Costs are assigned to the activities that are the cause of the overhead (known as cost pools) and then charged to the products that are actually demanding those activities (referred to as cost drivers).

Allocation: the portion of a company's overheads which can be charged directly to a cost centre.

Amortisation: similar to depreciation and usually applied to intangible non-current assets such as leases or goodwill, writing-off a non-current asset over time.

Apportionment: the process whereby costs are spread over various cost centres, for example according to floor area or headcount.

Appropriation account: the part of the income statement showing how ownership funds are dispersed.

Balanced scorecard: a strategy tool for measuring performance first devised by Kaplan and Norton, comprising financial, customer, internal and learning perspectives.

Break-even point: the activity level where the organisation is making neither profit nor loss, i.e., total revenues equal total costs.

Budget: a financial plan prepared prior to a defined period of time for the purpose of meeting specific objectives.

Capital expenditure: purchase of non-current assets such as buildings, machines or vehicles for business use.

Contribution: a measure of profit based on the difference between sales revenue and variable costs.

Cost centre: a location, function or group of activities for which costs can be attributed.

Cost of capital: the interest rate relating to the cost of funds used to finance a project.

Cost centre: a business unit or department that is responsible for the costs that it incurs.

Cost driver: the factor causing a change in an activity's cost.

Cost pool: a collection of costs associated with a particular business activity or cost driver.

Depreciation: the decrease in value of a non-current asset over time through wear and tear.

Direct labour: the labour costs, usually in the form of wages, associated with shop-floor staff involved with the conversion process of a product or service.

Direct materials: raw materials which can be assigned to the production of a good or service.

Financial accounting: the preparation of financial statements to external users of information, primarily shareholders.

Financial ratio: the relationship between two or more financial values, expressed as a percentage, fraction or ratio.

Financial statements: (also referred to as final accounts) the income statement, statement of cash flows and statement of financial position.

Fixed assets: (now called non-current assets) the assets a business needs to carry out trade such as buildings, machines and vehicles.

Fixed costs: costs which are unaffected by the level of activity, such as rent.

Gearing: refers to the balance sheet funding provided by sources other than the owners.

Goodwill: classed as an intangible asset, it shows the difference between the amount paid for an enterprise and the net value of the assets acquired.

Indirect costs: (or overheads) costs not directly related to the production of a good or a service, such as administrative salaries or depreciation.

Intangible assets: assets which have value but are not physical in nature, such as intellectual property, patent rights, brands and goodwill.

Internal rate of return (IRR): a project appraisal technique showing the rate of return achieved when the sum of the discounted cash flows is equal to the original capital outlay, i.e., the net present value is zero.

Inventories: (also known as stock or stock-in-trade) raw materials, work-in-progress and finished goods, usually shown at the lower of cost or market value.

Investment appraisal: (also known as project appraisal or capital budgeting) is a collection of techniques, such as payback, NPV (Net Present Value) or IRR, used to identify the attractiveness of an *investment*.

Key performance indicator (KPI): a measurable value that demonstrates how effectively a company is achieving key business objectives.

Long-term liabilities: (now known as non-current liabilities) debt which is not due for repayment for a year or more.

Management accounting: financial information intended mainly for the benefit of managers.

Marginal costing: an accounting method that calculates the costs of a product or service by considering only the variable costs.

Master budget: the overall summary of an organisation's plans, comprising forecast income statement, cash flows and financial position.

Net present value (NPV): a highly regarded investment appraisal technique which uses discounted cash flow to show the sum of the present values of incoming and outgoing cash flows over time.

Overheads: (or indirect costs) costs not directly related to the production of a good or a service, such as administrative salaries or straight-line depreciation.

Payback: the time taken for the cash flows of a capital project to equal the original outlay, normally expressed in years.

Prime costs: the direct costs of a commodity in terms of materials and labour.

Profit: revenue minus costs.

Profit centre: a business unit or department within an organisation that generates revenues and profits or losses.

Purchases: items bought for the purpose of re-sale.

Responsibility accounting: the reporting and analysis of financial information about decision centres within an organisation.

Sales: income derived from the principal activity of an organisation by exchanging goods or services for money, usually shown net of VAT.

Standard cost: the estimated cost of performing an operation or producing a good under normal conditions.

Variable costs: costs which increase as the level of activity goes up, such as direct materials.

Variance analysis: a key element of performance management whereby the difference between budgeted and actual costs is calculated and explained.

Work-in-progress: the value of partly completed manufactured goods.

Working capital: (also known as net current assets) current assets minus current liabilities.

Chapter 2	
1	a
2	c
3	b
4	c
5	d
6	c
7	a
8	c
9	c
10	b
11	b
12	d
13	a
14	b
15	a
16	d
17	d
18	b
19	c
20	c
21	b
22	d
23	b
24	c
25	d
26	d
27	c
28	c
29	a
30	a

Chapter 4	
1	a
2	c
3	c
4	c
5	b
6	a
Chapter 5	
1	a
2	b
3	b
4	b
5	b
6	b

www.ingramcontent.com/pod-product-compliance
Lightning Source LLC
Chambersburg PA
CBHW070914260726
48661CB00004B/1728